# Fish Colours

Mary Walker

RIGBY

This fish has red scales.

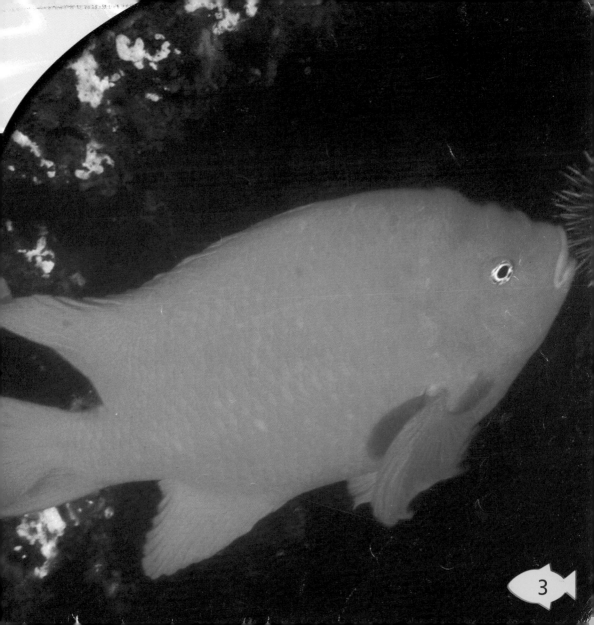

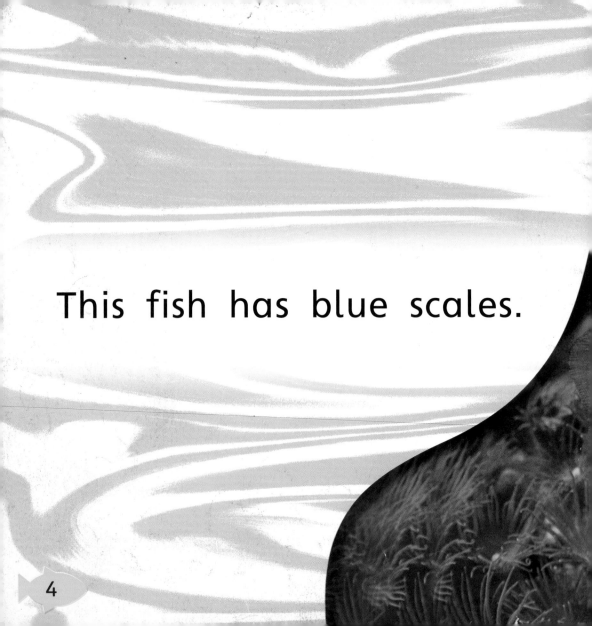

This fish has blue scales.

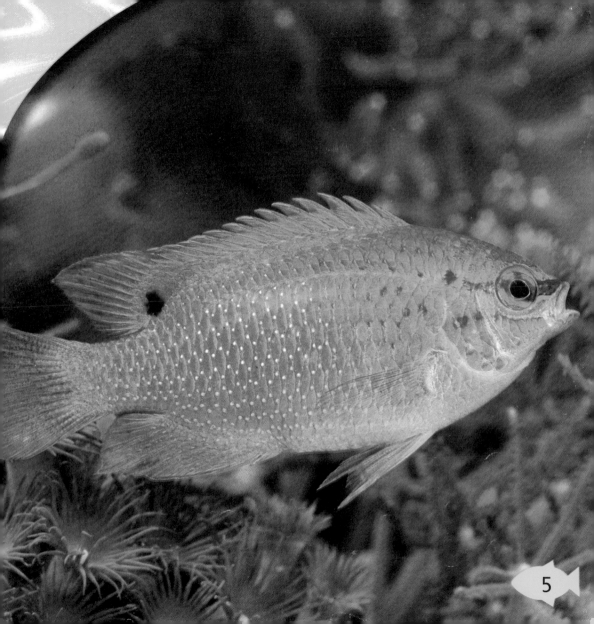

5

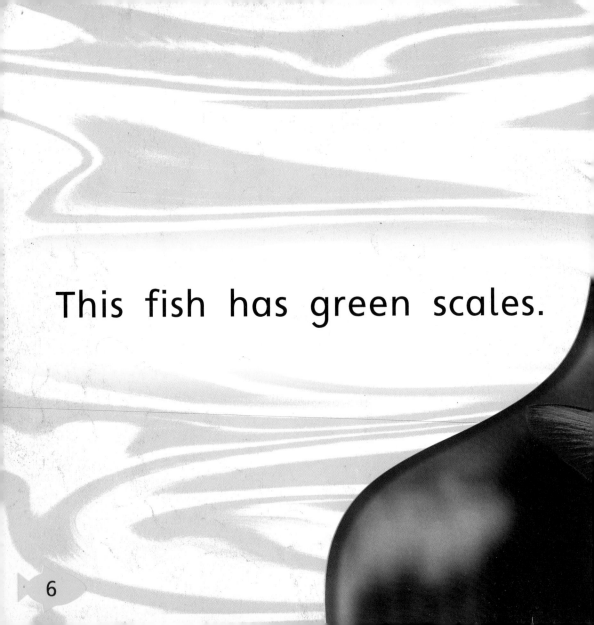

This fish has green scales.

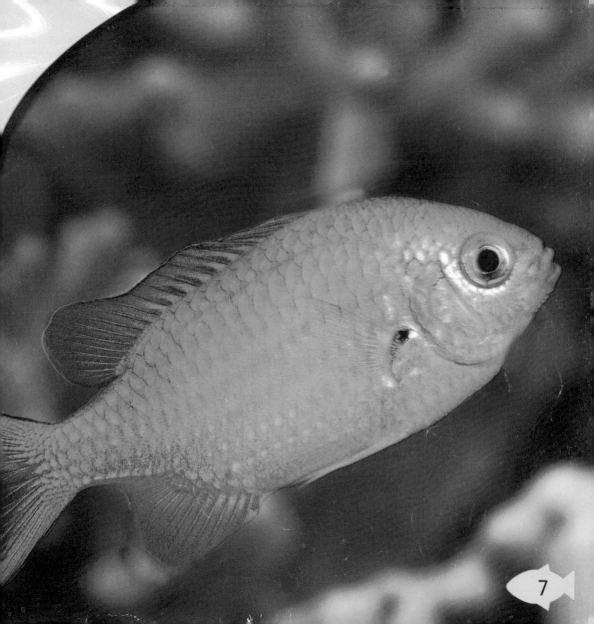

This fish has yellow scales.

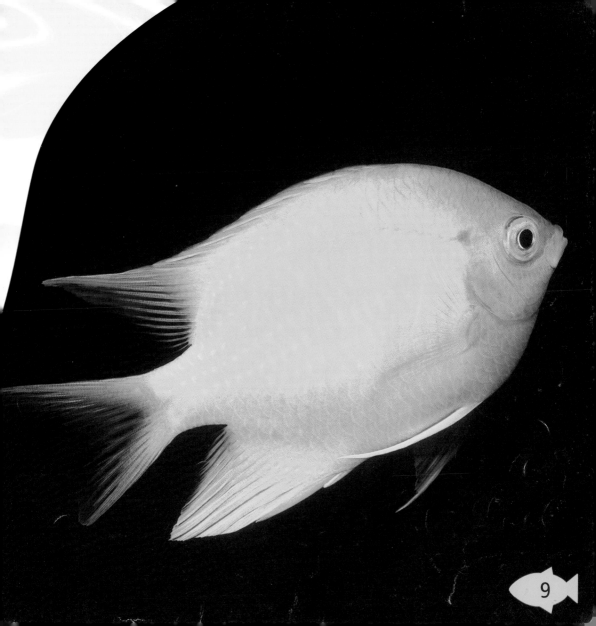

# Look at this fish.

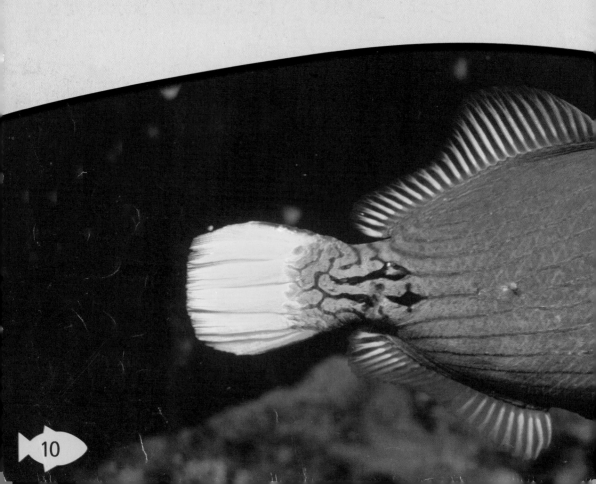

This fish has red, blue, green and yellow scales!

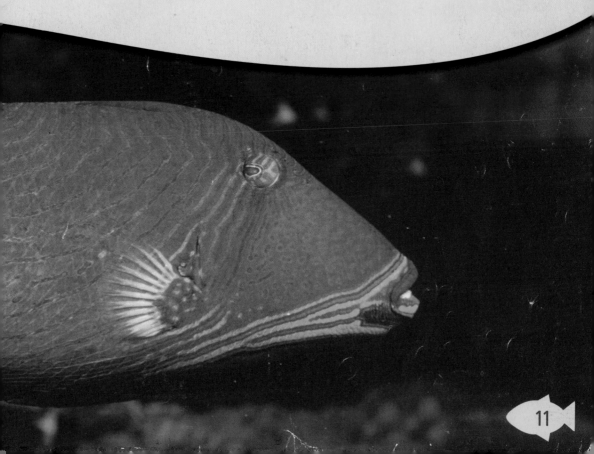

# Index

12